The Good Traveller

Luke 10: God Saves

CATHERINE MACKENZIE
Illustrated by Chiara Bertelli

**Learn it: Only God can give eternal life
Do it: Ask God for mercy. Show mercy.
Find it: How does God show love? Romans 5:8**

Do you have to be nice to everyone? If someone is nasty to you, should you be nasty back? If people are different to us, how should we treat them?

One day, Jesus met a lawyer who asked questions like this, but the lawyer's first question was quite different.

He asked Jesus, 'Teacher, what shall I do to inherit eternal life?' Jesus decided to answer this question with a question.

He asked, 'What does the Word of God say?' The lawyer replied,

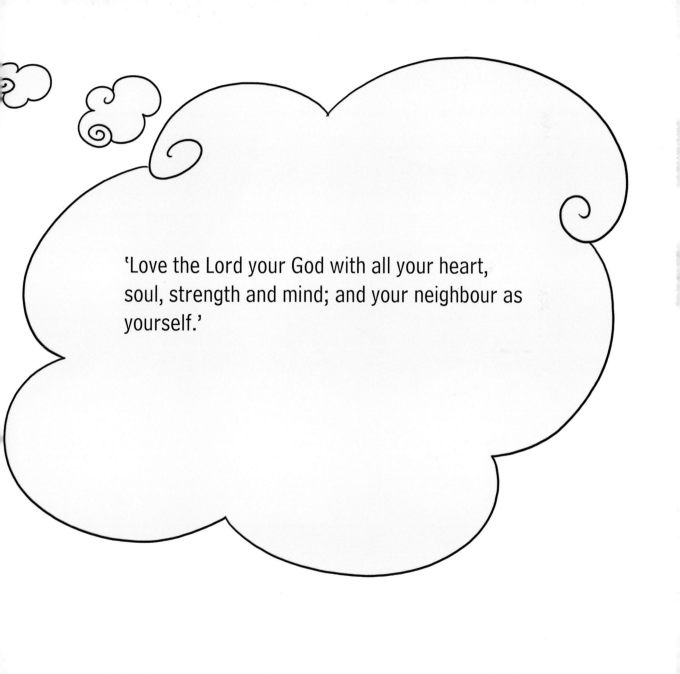

'Love the Lord your God with all your heart, soul, strength and mind; and your neighbour as yourself.'

Jesus said to him, 'That's correct. If you do this you will live.' But the lawyer knew this was difficult. He wanted it to be easy. So he tried to wiggle out of the problem by asking Jesus, 'Who is my neighbour?'

Perhaps he just wanted to be nice to his friends?

That's when Jesus told a story...

One day, a Jewish traveller was attacked by robbers. They left him for dead. A Jewish priest discovered him, but passed by. Another Jewish leader also saw the injured man and did nothing.

Both of these men knew that God wants us to help others. But they didn't do anything.

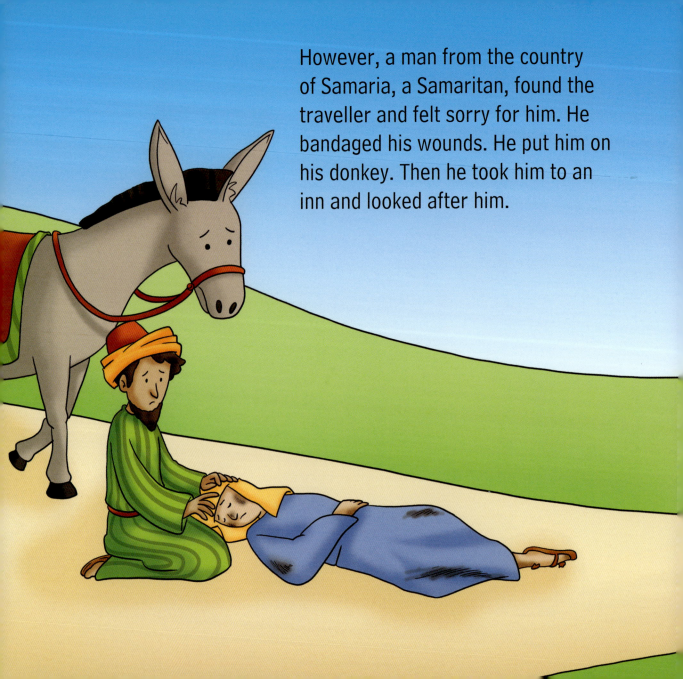

However, a man from the country of Samaria, a Samaritan, found the traveller and felt sorry for him. He bandaged his wounds. He put him on his donkey. Then he took him to an inn and looked after him.

The next day he paid the innkeeper and said, 'Take care of him. If you need more money, I'll pay you when I get back.'

Jesus then asked the lawyer, 'Who was a true neighbour to the injured traveller?' Now the Jews and the Samaritans didn't like each other.

They often had big arguments with one another. But the Jewish lawyer could see that the neighbour and hero of Jesus' story was the Samaritan who had looked after the traveller.

So the lawyer said to Jesus, 'The one who showed mercy was the neighbour.' Jesus told the lawyer to go and do the same. He was to show mercy to everyone, not just his friends.

He was to show mercy to people who were even his enemies.
It was a harder task than the lawyer had imagined.

Jesus wants us to realise that no human being can get to heaven by themselves. Our sin keeps us out. We might look good most of the time. We might be good some of the time.

But even then our good actions aren't good enough. If we are to get eternal life, we have to be given it by God.

The priest and the leader put themselves first. The Good Samaritan put the injured traveller first.

Jesus is the only one who is perfect and without sin. He is like the Good Samaritan.

Later in Jesus' life, he put himself last by dying on the cross and taking the punishment for sin.

QUESTION AND ANSWER:
WHAT IS MERCY?

MERCY is when you do something good for someone else who doesn't deserve it. If someone deserves to be punished but is set free then they are being shown mercy. God shows us mercy when he forgives us for the wrong things we do. We all displease God, so God is angry with us. But those who trust in God's Son, Jesus Christ, are freed from God's anger. God is merciful to them.

Jesus was willing to save people who did not love him and who were in fact his enemies. We are God's enemies if we don't turn away from our sin to trust God.

If you come to God for forgiveness, you are given Christ's goodness. That's how God's enemies become his friends.

Those who trust in Christ must live like Christ. Everyone is our neighbour. We should be kind and caring to people no matter where they come from or what they look like.

When Jesus has been merciful to us, we must be merciful to others. Trust in him for salvation and ask him to help you be like him.

Christian Focus Publications

Christian Focus Publications publishes books for adults and children under its four main imprints: Christian Focus, CF4K, Mentor and Christian Heritage. Our books reflect our conviction that God's Word is reliable and Jesus is the way to know him, and live for ever with him. Our children's list includes a Sunday School curriculum that covers pre-school to early teens, and puzzle and activity books. We also publish personal and family devotional titles, biographies and inspirational stories that children will love. If you are looking for quality Bible teaching for children then we have an excellent range of Bible stories and age-specific theological books. From pre-school board books to teenage apologetics, we have it covered!

AUTHOR'S DEDICATON: To my friends and family at Kingsview Christian Centre, A.P.C.

10 9 8 7 6 5 4 3 2 1

Copyright © 2016 Catherine Mackenzie

ISBN: 978-1-78191-754-1

Published in 2016 by Christian Focus Publications Ltd.

Geanies House, Fearn, Tain, Ross-shire, IV20 1TW, Great Britain

Illustrations by Chiara Bertelli

Cover Design: Sarah Bosman

Printed in China

When Jesus has been merciful to us, we must be merciful to others. Trust in him for salvation and ask him to help you be like him.

Christian Focus Publications

Christian Focus Publications publishes books for adults and children under its four main imprints: Christian Focus, CF4K, Mentor and Christian Heritage. Our books reflect our conviction that God's Word is reliable and Jesus is the way to know him, and live for ever with him. Our children's list includes a Sunday School curriculum that covers pre-school to early teens, and puzzle and activity books. We also publish personal and family devotional titles, biographies and inspirational stories that children will love. If you are looking for quality Bible teaching for children then we have an excellent range of Bible stories and age-specific theological books. From pre-school board books to teenage apologetics, we have it covered!

AUTHOR'S DEDICATON: To my friends and family at Kingsview Christian Centre, A.P.C.

10 9 8 7 6 5 4 3 2 1

Copyright © 2016 Catherine Mackenzie

ISBN: 978-1-78191-754-1

Published in 2016 by Christian Focus Publications Ltd.

Geanies House, Fearn, Tain, Ross-shire, IV20 1TW, Great Britain

Illustrations by Chiara Bertelli

Cover Design: Sarah Bosman

Printed in China